An interview with Florence Nightingale

Contents

An interview with Florence Nightingale 2

Florence's early life..4

Florence wants to be a nurse.........................6

Florence trains to be a nurse 8

Florence hears about the Crimean War 10

Florence goes to the Crimean War................12

The Lady with the Lamp 14

Florence comes home 16

Florence and her work 18

The future for Florence 20

Florence's later life 22

Index 24

An interview with Florence Nightingale

Florence Nightingale worked as a nurse in the 1800s. Over 150 years later she is still the most famous nurse in Britain. Read this imaginary interview with Florence Nightingale to find out why people still remember her today.

The interview takes place in 1860. The interviewer asks Florence questions about her life and work.

▲ The interviewer

▲ Florence Nightingale

▲ Florence Nightingale

Florence's early life

 **Where did you grow up and what was it like?**

 My parents had a lot of money. I lived in a big house called Embley Park, near London. I did not go to school, but my father gave me lessons at home. My favourite lesson was maths.

◀ Embley Park

 **Did you always want to be a nurse?**

When I was young, I knew I wanted to help people. I used to practise first aid on my pet dog.

▲ Richard Monckton Milnes wanted to marry Florence

As I grew up, I believed that God wanted me to care for people. Many young men wanted to marry me, but I said no. I wanted to become a nurse.

Florence wants to be a nurse

What did your parents think about you wanting to be a nurse?

My parents were very angry. They did not think a lady from a rich family should have a job. My mother fainted. She did not want me to work in a hospital.

Why did your parents try to stop you?

The hospitals were dirty and crowded. Most nurses came from poor homes and did not know how to look after sick people. Some nurses were lazy and dirty.

▲ A cartoon of a nurse in the 1840s

▼ Hospitals in the early 1800s were crowded and dirty

Florence trains to be a nurse

How did you become a nurse?

I visited a hospital in Germany when I was on holiday with friends in 1850. The hospital was clean and the nurses knew how to look after sick people. I knew that was where I wanted to train to be a nurse. I went back to Germany to train for three months in 1851.

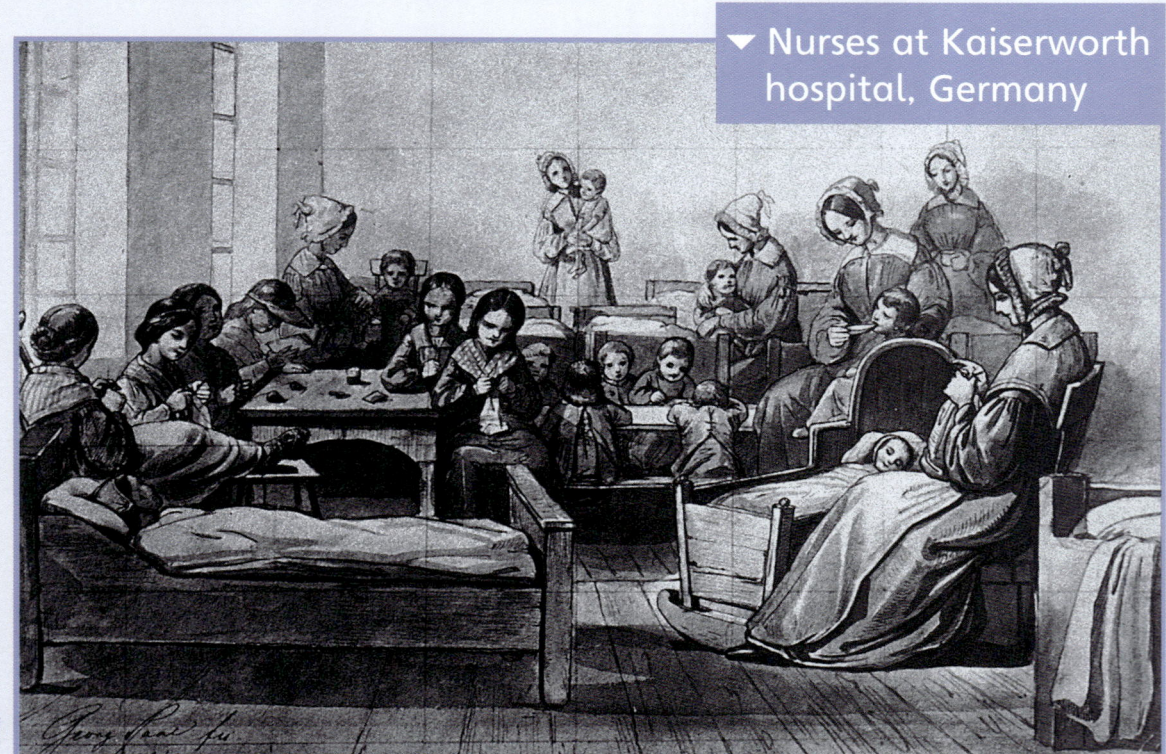

▼ Nurses at Kaiserworth hospital, Germany

What did you do after your training?

I came back to England after my training. My parents still did not want me to be a nurse. But, in the end my father said I could help run a small hospital in London.

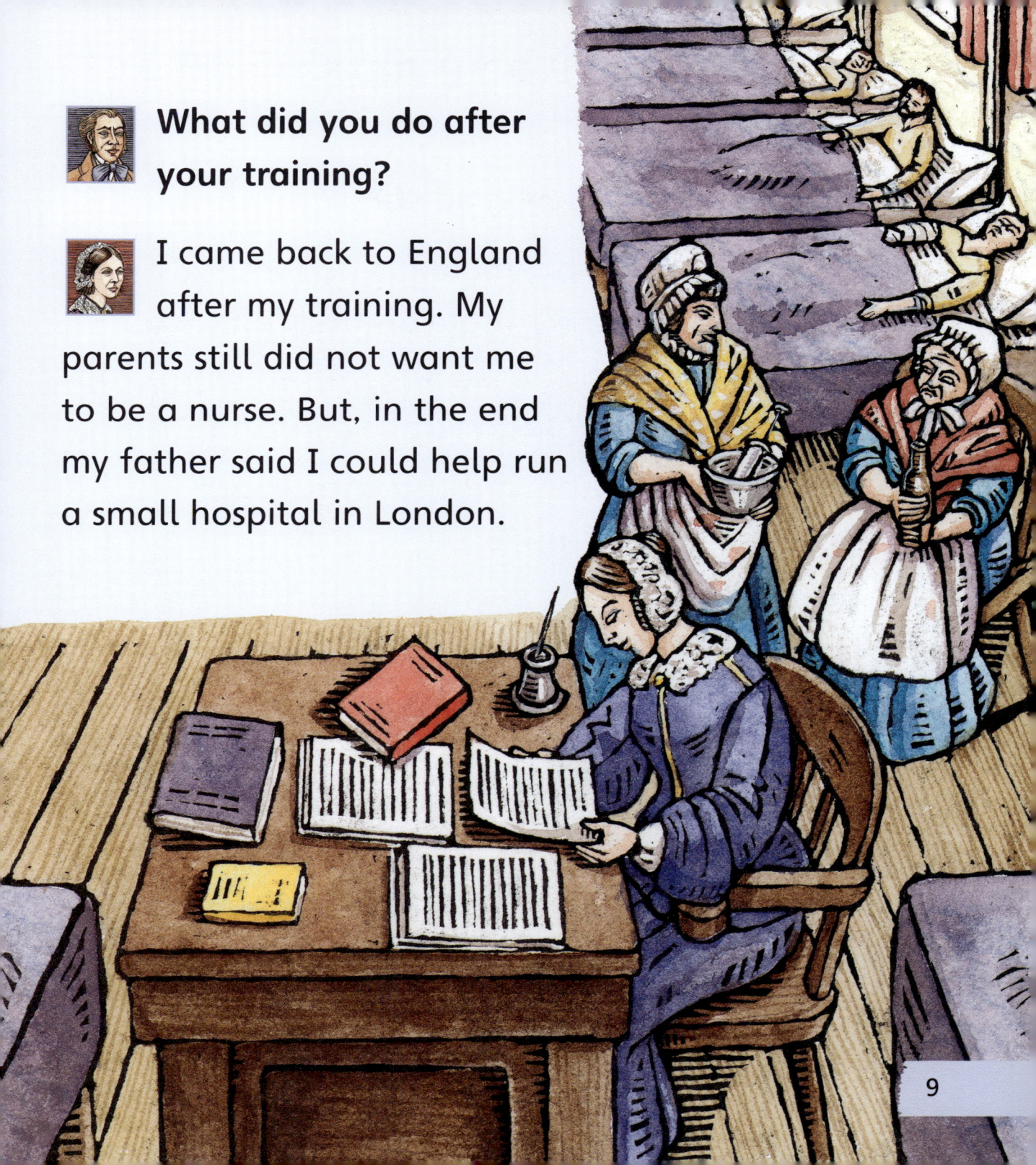

Florence hears about the Crimean War

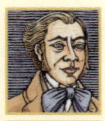

How did you hear about the Crimean War?

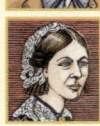

My friends and family told me about the Crimean War in Russia. Russian soldiers and British soldiers were fighting each other with guns and cannons. *The Times* newspaper reported that many British soldiers were badly hurt.

▼ *The Times*, 1854

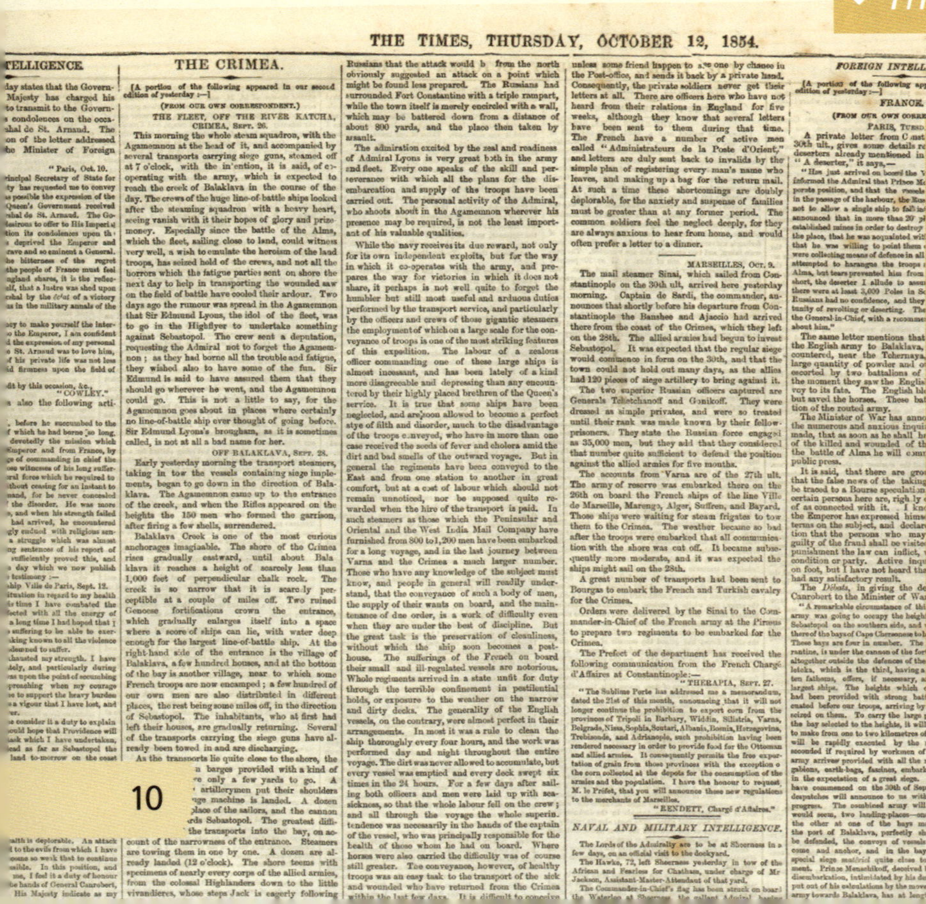

THE TIMES, THURSDAY, OCTOBER 12, 1854. 7

INTELLIGENCE

THE CRIMEA.

FOREIGN INTELLIGENCE.

FRANCE.

NAVAL AND MILITARY INTELLIGENCE.

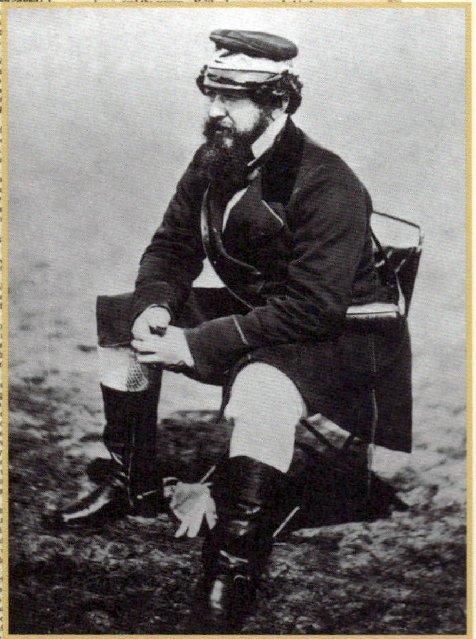

▲ A journalist in the Crimea, 1854

How did it make you feel?

I was very worried. There weren't any nurses to look after the soldiers. *The Times* reported that the army hospitals were dirty and full of germs. The British Government knew about my work in London and asked me to help. I agreed and gave up my job at the hospital straight away.

▼ A painting of the Crimean War, 1854

Florence goes to the Crimean War

Where did you go to help?

Most of the injured soldiers were being sent to the army hospital in Scutari, Turkey. They went there to be safe from Russian attack. I sailed to Turkey with 38 nurses on 23 October 1854.

▲ Florence set sail on the *Vectis*

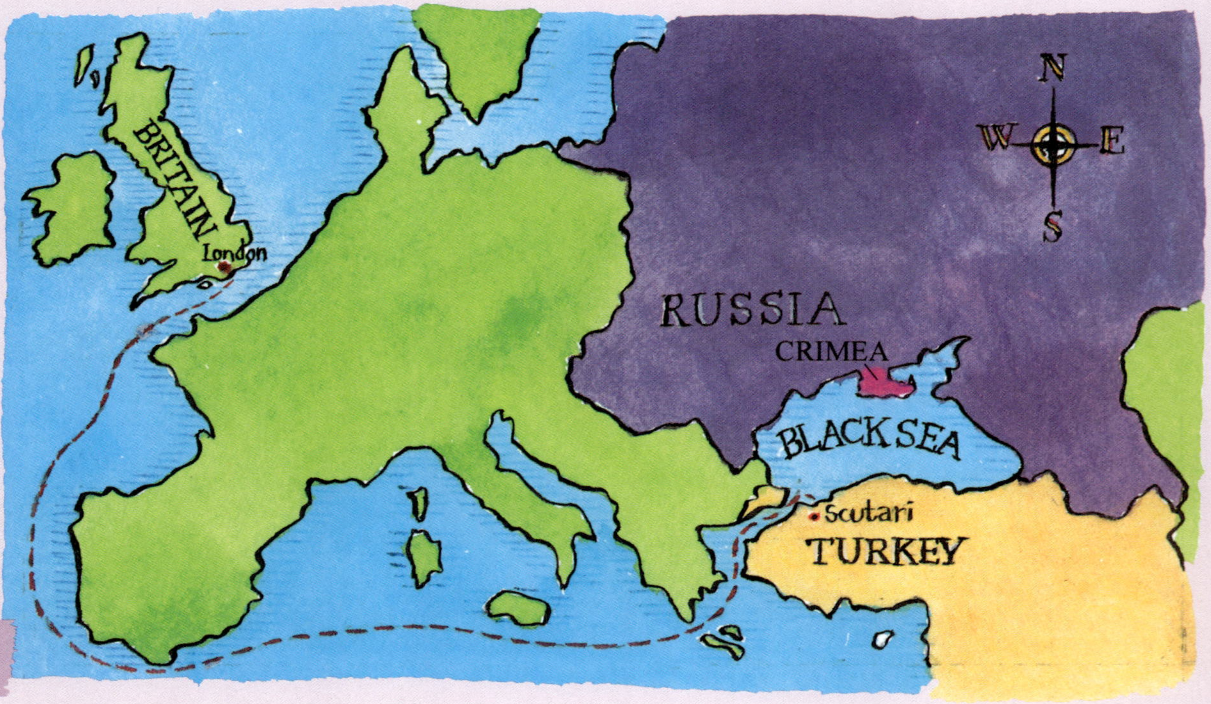

 **What was the army hospital like when you arrived?**

Many British soldiers were dying. The hospital was dirty and there was no clean water. I kept records of the number of soldiers who died. I wrote letters to the British Government asking for help.

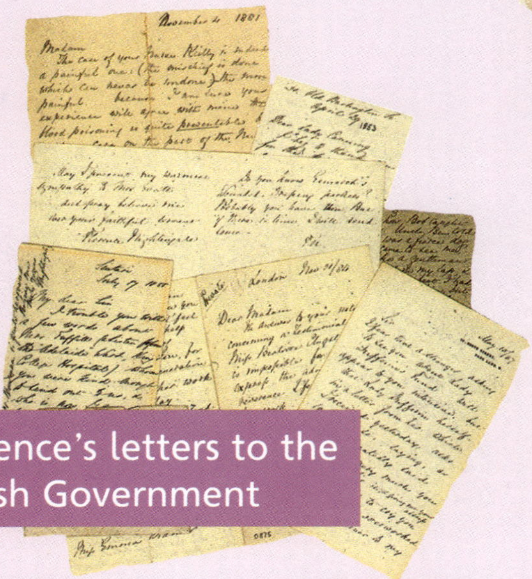

▲ Florence's letters to the British Government

The Lady with the Lamp

What did you and your nurses do to help?

We worked very hard to clean up the hospital. We dressed the soldiers' wounds and gave them medicine to help with their pain. At first, the army doctors did not want us there. When they saw how much we could do to help, they soon changed their minds.

▲ Florence's medical chest

▼ The army hospital in Scutari

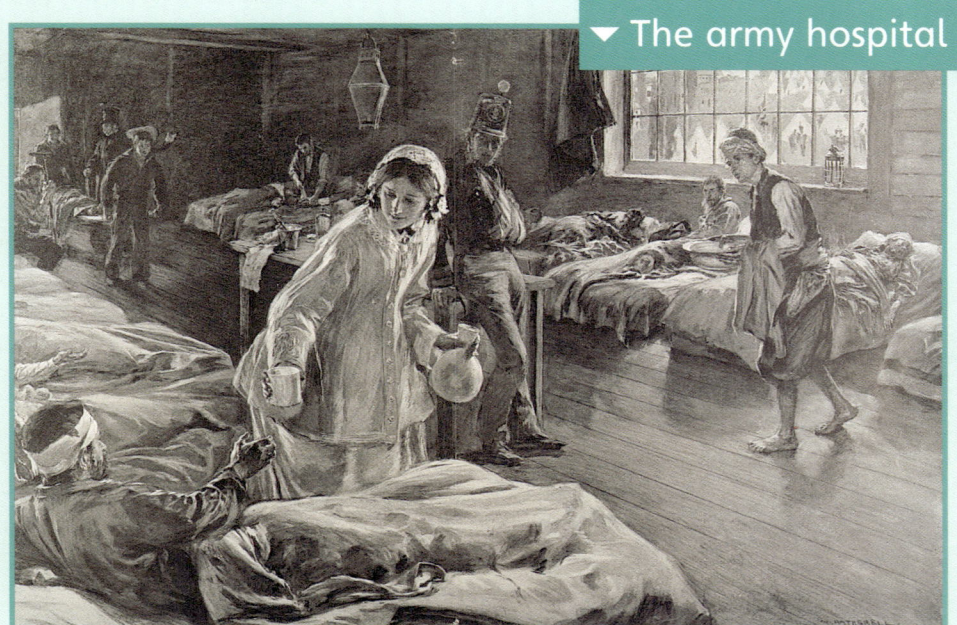

How did the army hospital improve?

We got cleaner water and fewer soldiers died. I walked around the hospital at night with a lamp and talked to soldiers who could not sleep. The nurses helped to write letters for the soldiers and read books to them.

▲ Florence's lamp

▼ Soldiers called Florence 'The Lady with the Lamp'

Florence comes home

 **What happened when you came back to Britain?**

 I came back home just before the end of the war in 1856. I was invited to meet Queen Victoria. I told her about the problems in the army hospitals. She gave me a brooch for the work I had done in the Crimea.

▲ Brooch given by Queen Victoria

What was it like to be home?

It was good to be home but I did not like being famous. I felt tired and ill. I had important work to do for the army hospitals. I wanted peace and quiet to get on with my work.

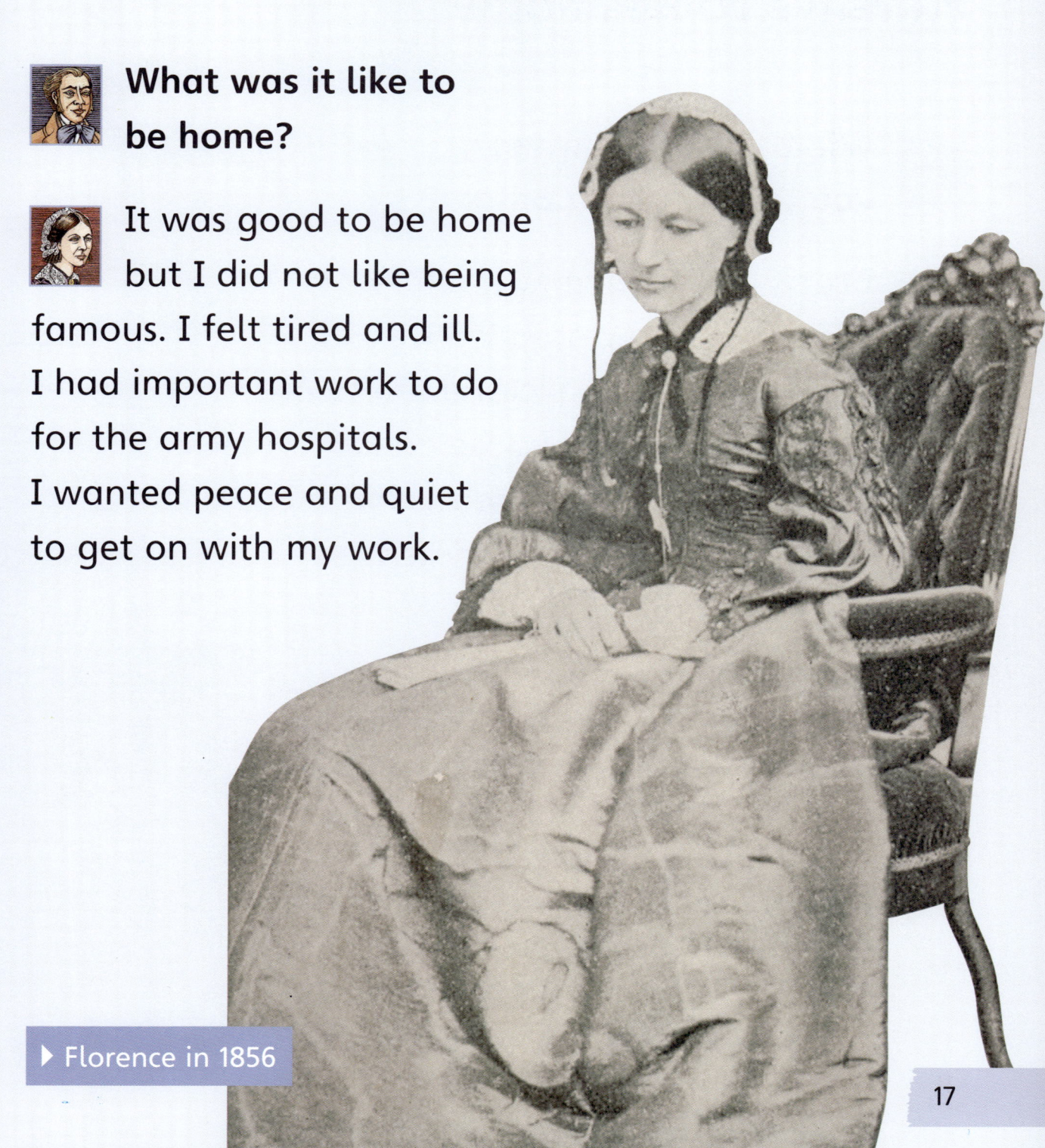

▶ Florence in 1856

Florence and her work

 **What did you do to help the army hospitals?**

I worked for the British Government. We looked at how the army organised its hospitals. I wrote a report explaining that most people died because the army hospitals were dirty and full of germs. The army agreed to give the soldiers better food and cleaner beds.

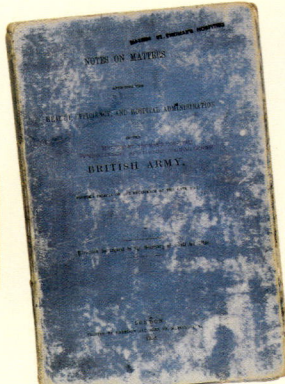

▸ Florence's report for the army hospitals

 **I hear you have also written a book. What's it about?**

It is called *Notes on Nursing*. I wanted to help people who could not afford to go to hospital. My book explains how to look after sick people at home.

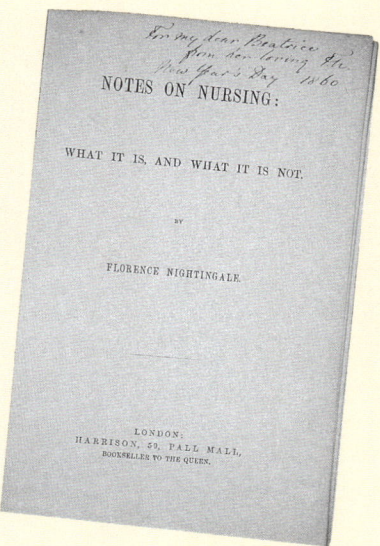

▲ Notes on Nursing

▲ Florence's pen, ink-bottle and writing box

The future for Florence

What are you working on now?

I am setting up schools to train new nurses. The schools are going to be in hospitals in big cities. I hope student nurses will learn by watching doctors and senior nurses.

▼ St Thomas's Hospital, London

What are your plans for the future?

In Turkey the dirt in the army hospitals killed thousands of British soldiers. Dirt is killing many people in Britain too. I want to explain that they must keep clean to stay healthy.

▼ Dirty streets in Britain in the 1850s

Florence's later life

In later life, Florence Nightingale continued to help train nurses. She went blind in 1895 but she did not stop writing books and giving advice. Florence Nightingale died in 1910, but her work to improve hospitals is still remembered today.

▼ Florence and her nurses in 1886

Florence Nightingale

1820	Born in Florence, Italy. First person ever to be named Florence, after the city.
1851	Goes to Germany to become a nurse.
1853	Starts work at a hospital in London.
1854	The Crimean War begins. Goes with her nurses to the army hospital in Turkey.
1856	Comes back to Britain. The Crimean War ends.
1860	*Notes on Nursing* is published.
	The Nightingale School for Nurses opens at St Thomas's Hospital in London.
1883	Awarded the Royal Red Cross.
1908	Given the Freedom of the City of London.
1910	Dies at the age of 90.

Index

army 11, 12, 13, 14, 15, 16, 17, 18, 21, 23

British Government 11, 13, 18

brooch..16

Crimean War 10, 11, 12, 23

doctors 14

germs 11, 18

Lady with the Lamp 14, 15

Notes on Nursing 19, 23

nurse 2, 5, 6, 7, 8, 9, 11, 12, 14, 15, 20, 22, 23

Queen Victoria 16

Scutari 12, 14

soldiers.....................10, 11, 12, 13, 14, 15, 18, 21

The Times..10, 11

Turkey...12, 21, 23